Additional Praise for

CAPTURING CRITICAL KNOWLEDGE FROM A SHIFTING WORK FORCE

"Organizations that successfully harness their own knowledge bases (explicit and tacit) tend to remain competitive in global markets. This book is more than a primer in offering a systematic approach on how best to identify, target, capture, and share tacit, critical knowledge within an organization that would otherwise be lost when key individuals retire or leave the group. The recommendations and lessons learned from the best practices of several multinational organizations are well documented by APQC. This is an important read for those interested in harnessing their knowledge bases."

— *A. Rahman Khan, Knowledge Management Architect at Intel Corporation*

Praise For Other Books From APQC

KNOWLEDGE MANAGEMENT: A GUIDE FOR YOUR JOURNEY TO BEST-PRACTICE PROCESSES

"APQC has built an outstanding reputation for making complex subject areas meaningful, understandable, and actionable. APQC's Passport to Success book on knowledge management continues this rich tradition. ... This publication is helping us leverage the collective intellect of practitioners in this field."

— *Bipin Junnarkar, Vice President of Knowledge Management and Chief Knowledge Office at Gateway Inc.*

STAGES OF IMPLEMENTATION: A GUIDE FOR YOUR JOURNEY TO KM BEST PRACTICES

"A crisp summary of KM implementation best practices and lessons learned from leading companies across a range of industries. This book is essential reading for knowledge managers and business managers alike."

— *Reid Smith, Vice President of Knowledge Management at Schlumberger Limited*

CAPTURING CRITICAL KNOWLEDGE
FROM A SHIFTING WORK FORCE

Alice Haytmanek

Paige Leavitt

Darcy Lemons

APQC®
AMERICAN PRODUCTIVITY
& QUALITY CENTER

American Productivity & Quality Center
123 North Post Oak Lane, Third Floor
Houston, Texas 77024

Copyright © 2003 by American Productivity & Quality Center
All rights reserved, including the right of reproduction in whole or in part in any form.

Edited by Emma Skogstad
Designed by Connie Choate

Manufactured in the United States of America

ISBN 1-928593-83-6

American Productivity & Quality Center
Web site address: www.apqc.org

Table of Contents

Acknowledgements 4
Introduction 5
Chapter 1: Knowledge Management Background and Stages ... 7
Chapter 2: Types of Knowledge 15
Chapter 3: Identify and Share Critical Knowledge 19
Chapter 4: Support Structures and Funding 37
Chapter 5: Critical Success Factors 43
Chapter 6: Conclusion 47

About the Authors 51
About APQC 53

Acknowledgements

The American Productivity & Quality Center (APQC) would like to thank all of the organizations we have worked with to uncover the trends and best practices in knowledge management. Without the companies that sponsor our research—and especially those that are willing to impart their knowledge, experiences, and insights—we would not be able to share this valuable knowledge with the public.

We extend a special thank-you to those organizations that sponsored the consortium benchmarking study, Retaining Valuable Knowledge, as well as those that participated as partner organizations and allowed our study team to examine and learn from their knowledge retention practices. Information in this book was gained during this consortium benchmarking forum.

Introduction

The days of necessity are upon many organizations. Retirement, specifically, is having an injurious effect on organizations already destabilized by an uncertain economy. Such trends can lead to a great loss in an organization's collective knowledge, and retirement is not the only factor impacting knowledge attrition. Rapid growth, turnover, mergers and acquisitions, and internal redeployment also create knowledge gaps. The large majority of employees have been with their current employer less than four years.

Maintaining a knowledgeable work force is of major importance, but it can be a difficult issue, especially if senior management lacks awareness of the applicability of knowledge management. Yet the proven principles, tools, and practices of knowledge management can be systematically applied to capture departing knowledge and transfer it to new employees. A preemptive, strategically aligned knowledge capture and transfer system can counterbalance both inevitable and unforeseen challenges.

What can you do to prepare for those challenges?

And what can be done if circumstances are already less than ideal?

KNOWLEDGE RETENTION GUIDANCE

Organizations hold onto lessons learned through organized and pervasive knowledge management initiatives. Successful processes and tools can be deployed to better retain valuable knowledge.

APQC has found several successful approaches to retain valuable knowledge among organizations at different stages of their knowledge management journeys. Some organizations prepared a preemptive strike against oncoming losses. Others responded to damage felt from knowledge now lost. Valuable lessons can be learned from their responses, including how to:
- identify potential knowledge attrition,
- identify critical and inconsequential information,
- design and implement a knowledge management initiative,

- determine the necessary support structures and roles,
- determine the initiative's projected costs,
- identify implementation challenges, and
- measure the effectiveness of knowledge retention strategies.

This book will focus on determining types of knowledge, identifying and sharing critical knowledge, supporting structures and funding, and identifying critical success factors in knowledge retention. With vital information for both senior management and knowledge management practitioners, this book will detail the knowledge retention process, including indicators of a knowledge retention problem, necessary resources, realistic ways to capture knowledge, and processes to disseminate relevant information.

— Chapter 1 —

Knowledge Management Background and Stages

APQC has been identifying, studying, and sharing KM best practices for almost a decade. During its research into emerging trends, the Center has found consistently effective principals to manage a successful KM initiative. This book is based on the following tenets.

Knowledge management is a systematic process of connecting people to each other and to the information they need to effectively act. Knowledge management initiatives are intended to enhance performance through the identification, capture, validation, and transfer of knowledge.

APQC has found that most people want to share what they know and avoid others' mistakes. But employees are impeded by a lack of time, a cumbersome process, and questionable sources.

Some of these barriers are alleviated by technology, but applications are not the solution. Technology applications do not, in themselves, create a need or demand to change behavior or share knowledge. It is critical to select and implement technology as part of a larger, systematic knowledge management change initiative.

Senior executive support also alleviates barriers to sharing knowledge by encouraging appropriate behavior and embracing new approaches. Employee support follows if knowledge management principles and tools are applied to important business issues. Fostering a knowledge-sharing culture is the result of a successful knowledge management strategy. It is not a prerequisite.

Most importantly, knowledge must be embedded in employees' work flow so that it can be captured, shared, and reused during daily responsibilities. By providing value to those who participate, employees experience greater professional development. Of course, rewards and recognition are important, but they will not take the place of knowledge-sharing systems that work and provide value.

In addition to these basic tenets, APQC has found that knowledge management—and knowledge retention—occur in five developmental stages.

KNOWLEDGE RETENTION ACROSS THE STAGES OF KM

Establishing a knowledge retention strategy can be a daunting task. Getting started down the right path is often difficult, and staying on course can be even more so as roadblocks emerge. APQC's Road Map to Knowledge Management Results: Stages of Implementation™ illustrates how organizations can position themselves and determine what tasks and activities are appropriate at an enterprise level *(Figure 1)*. Every stage of KM implementation involves unique issues, tactics, tools, characteristics, requirements, and action steps. By completing the key activities for each stage,

> Every stage of KM implementation involves unique issues, tactics, tools, characteristics, requirements, and action steps.

organizations will maintain sound footing throughout the entire KM implementation process.

Not all organizations begin in Stage 1. Many organizations jumpstart to Stage 3 by assembling knowledge management projects and initiatives in a grassroots approach, without a formal strategy. This local response creates credible results with limited resources. However, the first two stages may need to be revisited for organization wide strategy development.

So that you will better understand how organizations successfully retain business-critical knowledge, the rest of this chapter will address knowledge retention efforts and approaches at each stage.

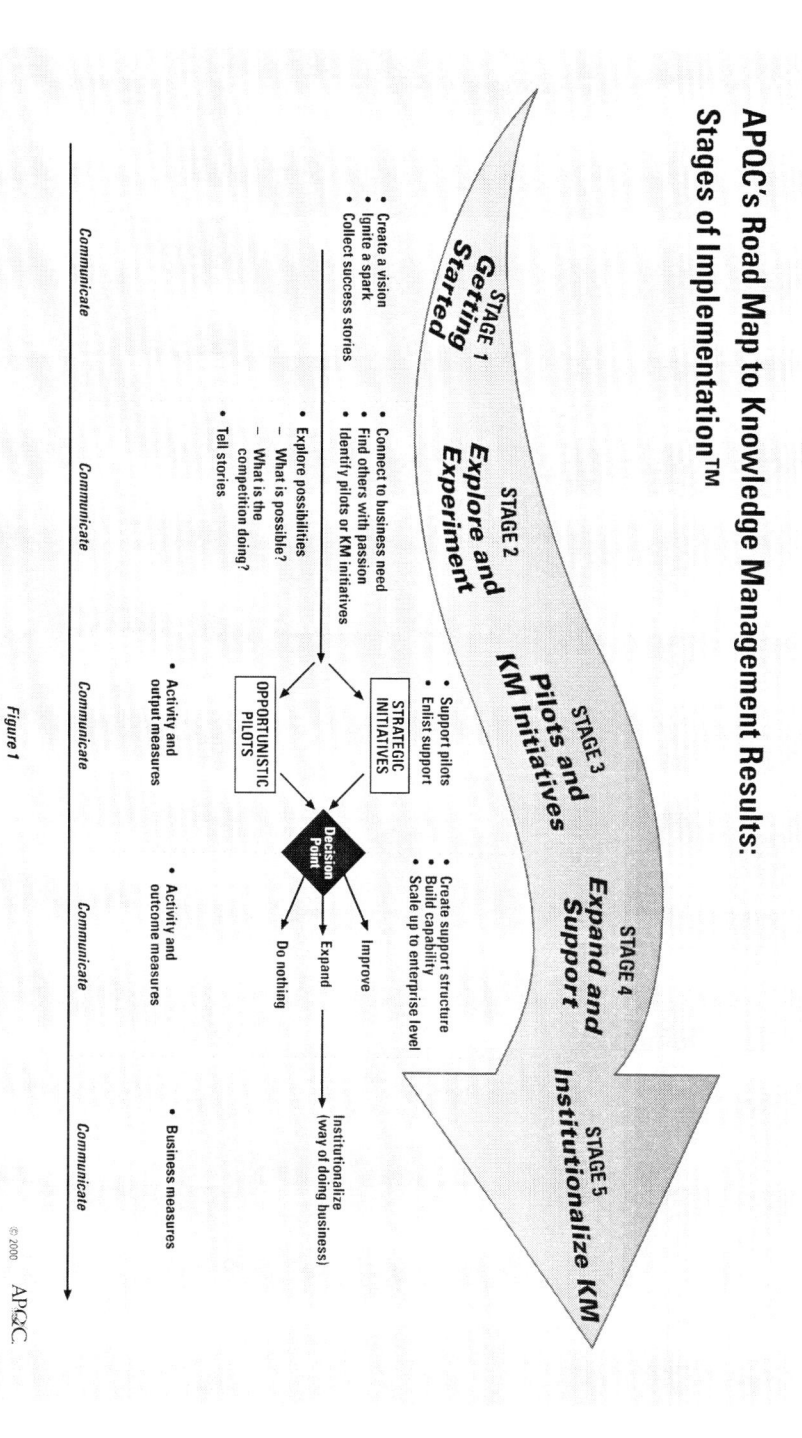

Knowledge Management Background and Stages | 9

APQC's Road Map to Knowledge Management Results:
Stages of Implementation™

STAGE 1 — Getting Started
- Create a vision
- Ignite a spark
- Collect success stories

STAGE 2 — Explore and Experiment
- Connect to business need
- Find others with passion
- Identify pilots or KM initiatives
- Explore possibilities
  - What is possible?
  - What is the competition doing?
- Tell stories

STAGE 3 — Pilots and KM Initiatives
- Support pilots
- Enlist support

STRATEGIC INITIATIVES
OPPORTUNISTIC PILOTS

Decision Point → Do nothing / Expand / Improve

STAGE 4 — Expand and Support
- Create support structure
- Build capability
- Scale up to enterprise level

STAGE 5 — Institutionalize KM
- Institutionalize (way of doing business)

Communicate → Communicate → Communicate → Communicate → Communicate

- Activity and output measures
- Activity and outcome measures
- Business measures

Figure 1

© 2000 APQC

Stage 1: Get Started

Many knowledge management efforts start with a single champion or small group of leaders who explore the concepts of knowledge management and understand the value to the organization. Unless the CEO or some other senior-level executive is the primary impetus behind early knowledge management efforts, the first stage will involve gaining senior management support.

To retain valuable knowledge, the most critical objectives in Stage 1 are to build the awareness of knowledge loss as a strategic issue and to tie efforts to corporate goals. As the original champion or group explores the potential impact of developing knowledge retention strategies, it should highlight the cost of lost knowledge and correlate the value of knowledge management approaches to the mitigation of anticipated costs and losses. Internal studies can assess pending knowledge loss in subject areas and place some economic value on that loss.

If leadership is not yet supportive of efforts to address knowledge loss, champions may want to identify a burning platform issue related to knowledge loss or an external best practices example in knowledge management. Interviews and discussions with key stakeholders can reveal windows of opportunities for pilots, as well as solutions to initial barriers and potential cross-functional team. Support must be followed by attention and resources applied to the problems.

Stage 2: Develop Strategy

Stage 2 is the turning point from individual interest or local efforts in knowledge management to an organizational experiment. Stage 2 is characterized by the decision to explore potential benefits of organizational action. The leaders brought together in Stage 1 may continue to play an important role, but within a formalized knowledge management leadership structure. The original champions have successfully cemented senior executive sponsorship so that they can designate cross-organizational leadership responsibilities and articulate their knowledge retention strategies.

> Champions may want to identify a burning platform issue related to knowledge loss or an external best practices example in knowledge management.

The central task at this stage is to create a business case that will detail the first iteration of the knowledge retention strategy and describe how knowledge management and knowledge retention efforts complement organizational goals. Also, the cross-organizational leadership team should organize pilots to test concepts and estimate resource requirements.

Formal knowledge retention strategies may focus on several different objectives, such as:
- building a knowledge-sharing culture,
- orienting new hires more quickly,
- capturing departing knowledge,
- capturing project lessons learned for reuse,
- preventing the loss of technical knowledge, and
- establishing mentor relationships.

Stage 3: Design and Launch KM Initiatives

Stage 3 typically begins with the design and kickoff of one or more knowledge management initiatives. These pilot projects should demonstrate that knowledge management will work and will positively impact organizational performance. For this reason, the initial pilot projects should be carefully selected and supported to ensure their success. The organization should also address the cultural and change management enablers that will ensure wider participation in knowledge-sharing activities.

In Stage 3, partner organizations use a variety of approaches to capture and share knowledge in their organizations, from Web-enabled work flow capture systems to communities of practice. This mixture of approaches reflects designed knowledge retention mechanisms that fit the particular needs and business objectives for each organization.

Processes for capturing knowledge must fit the culture of the organization. To ensure practices and knowledge are transferred effectively and make a difference, organizations must connect people who are able and willing to share their experiences. An organization cannot expect people to change the way they work without giving them a reason to do so. APQC has found that in a knowledge-friendly culture, several principles typically exist.

- People see the connection between sharing knowledge and the business purpose.
- Knowledge sharing is tightly linked to the core cultural values of the organization.
- There is strong management and peer pressure for people to collaborate and share.
- Knowledge sharing is integrated with people's work through knowledge-sharing events and routine work processes.
- Human networks have a facilitator who is responsible for the network and ensures that people participate.
- The rewards and recognition system is aligned with sharing knowledge.

> An organization cannot expect people to change the way they work without giving them a reason to do so.

People's behavior, and hence company culture, will change when a reason for knowledge sharing is articulated and the appropriate tools are readily available. An organization's success is a function of the people who make it work.

Stage 4: Expand and Support

By the time an organization reaches Stage 4, knowledge management has proved valuable enough through pilot projects to garner

> An organization's success is a function of
> the people who make it work.

the attention and resources needed to expand the project. Demand for knowledge management support by other parts of the organization tends to be high, which provides additional evidence of its value.

At this stage, knowledge management is on its way to being considered a strategic and necessary competency for the organization. Each organization must create a structure and dedicate resources to expand and sustain the initial knowledge management efforts. This structure may look very different across organizations, from formal governance structures to distributed virtual knowledge management teams.

The added costs and visibility of resources devoted to knowledge management and knowledge retention efforts will often require formal business evaluation and ROI justification. In Stage 4, the organization makes a conscious decision to invest in the expansion and continued support of knowledge management. Knowledge initiatives will be line items in budgets, and the business case for knowledge management becomes formalized.

In Stage 4, the organization also develops an expansion strategy. The advisory group will need to understand the critical issues facing the organization and then identify opportunities for expansion much the way the initial pilot projects were selected. The appropriate resources need to be allocated.

Another characteristic of Stage 4 is that knowledge retention and sharing are more likely to be built into existing or new business initiatives, such as by adding a knowledge capture component to a Six Sigma process. More formalized measurement systems will also be built to track the effects of knowledge retention efforts.

Stage 5: Institutionalize Knowledge Management

At Stage 5, sharing and using knowledge become part of the organization's way of doing business. This stage involves embedding

knowledge management into the business model and continuing to monitor the intensity of knowledge capture and sharing. Knowledge-infused organizations share several key characteristics:
- knowledge and collaboration are extended more thoroughly to customers and partners;
- knowledge capture, sharing, and reuse are built into work processes;
- portals customized to deliver just-in-time information matching the preferences and roles of individual employees become commonplace; and
- knowledge management is integrated with the organization's learning and human resource development strategies.

In Stage 5, the knowledge management team may act as an internal standards board and monitor progress across the organization.

Chapter 2

Types of Knowledge

Knowledge comes in two forms: explicit and tacit. Explicit knowledge can be documented; tacit knowledge, on the other hand, resides in the mind(s) of an individual or a collective group. Established organizations typically have enormous amounts of tacit and explicit knowledge, only some of which is valuable and durable enough to create a competitive advantage and justify the costs of managing it. The challenge is to determine, locate, capture, and then share critical knowledge. The approach to manage explicit knowledge is mechanical; tacit knowledge management is more difficult.

Best-practice organizations primarily focus on capturing knowledge related to their functional areas. This is because the results of capturing and sharing this knowledge is more easily discernable in time or cost savings and directly affects the bottom line. Examples of functional knowledge are:

- analyses of client and industry,
- best practices in core competency,
- business management,
- campaign or project work,
- competencies and solutions,
- customer relationships,
- direct practice experience,
- engineering and planning,
- factory processes,
- IT customer support,
- knowledge about how to serve clients,
- knowledge of countries,
- knowledge of the sector,
- Six Sigma experience,
- operations,
- plant maintenance and operations,
- process management,
- production,
- products and services knowledge,
- product knowledge,
- project management,
- research and development,
- research studies and customer analyses,
- selling expertise,
- exploration,
- technical and marketing knowledge, and
- technical competency.

TACIT KNOWLEDGE

It is cheaper and more effective to capture knowledge before its loss becomes a burning platform issue or before the work experience is unavailable. Consequently, best-practice organizations find it worth the challenge to cultivate tacit knowledge.

Tacit knowledge is very difficult to transfer; however, it provides context, which makes it meaningful and applicable. Tacit knowledge can be found through interactions with employees, customers, and vendors. This knowledge is hard to catalog, highly experiential, difficult to document in detail, and transitory. It is also the basis for judgment and informed action. Organizations concerned about knowledge loss fear that tacit knowledge has not been captured (made explicit) or transferred so that others may benefit from it.

Internal networks, documentation of the work flow or process, project milestone reviews, training, mentoring, videotaping, After-Action Reviews, and project milestone reviews are often used to capture tacit knowledge. Videotaping is an effective means of tacit knowledge capture, but it is not frequently used. Cost may be the prohibiting factor here, as videotapes are expensive to create and distribute. Apprenticeship and mentoring are also not used as often as their effectiveness would seem to warrant, again perhaps because of costs. Internal networks are frequently used and considered effective. It is important to note that the more effective approaches have a personal or face-to-face element.

EXPLICIT KNOWLEDGE

Explicit knowledge, formal and often codified, can be documented. This type of knowledge is found in:

- books and technical documents,
- formulas,
- project reports,
- contracts,
- process diagrams,
- lists of lessons learned,
- case studies,
- white papers,
- policy manuals,
- process maps, and
- work flows.

> It is cheaper and more effective to capture knowledge before its loss becomes a burning platform issue or before the work experience is unavailable.

Like tacit knowledge, explicit knowledge may not be useful without the context provided by experience. Although explicit knowledge is easily available, it works best coupled with tacit knowledge from a subject matter expert.

Many best-practice organizations rely heavily on collaboration tools, such as teleconferences and chat rooms, for capturing explicit knowledge. Other tools used to capture explicit knowledge include content management systems, document management systems, and shared folders or drives. Although decision support systems and knowledge maps are infrequently used, they are very effective approaches for explicit knowledge capture. Other effective approaches to capture explicit data are communities of practice (CoPs), engagement team databases, issues systems, idea capture systems, call resolution systems, intranet sites, and event-specific e-mails. A knowledge base, be it a database or a repository, is considered moderately effective and therefore used moderately. Personal Web pages, expert systems (artificial intelligence), and case-based reasoning systems are not necessarily effective. For many organizations, an employee development program may be the most effective approach. The extent of use and effectiveness of the approaches are compared in *Figure 2*, page 18, based on feedback from best-practice organizations.

Comparison of Extent of Use and Effectiveness of Approaches for Capturing Explicit Knowledge

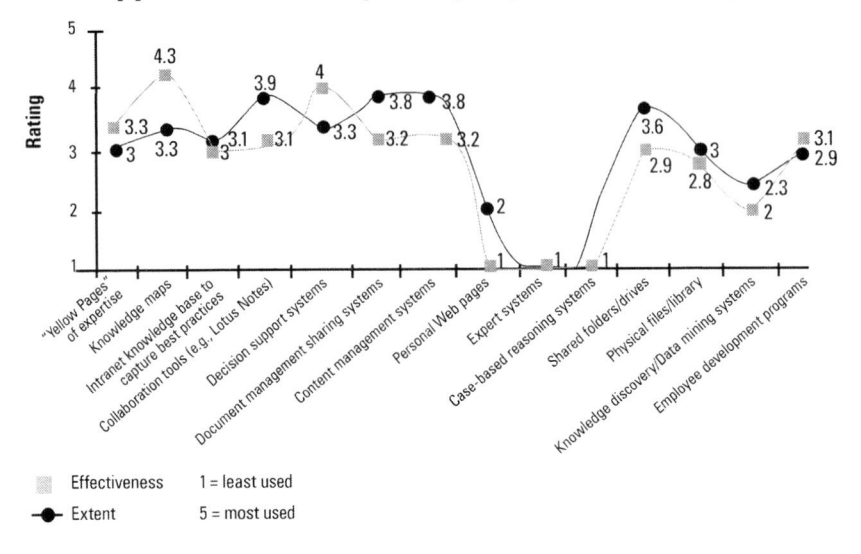

Figure 2

— Chapter 3 —

Identify and Share Critical Knowledge

Success stories surrounding knowledge management abound, making it easy for organizations to forget that not all knowledge is worth capturing, storing, and sharing. In fact, a knowledge retention initiative's success depends on the organization's ability to determine what is critical knowledge, how people could benefit from using it in a different way, and if the value proposition for this knowledge can be articulated.

An organization can have vast stores of information in its databases and filing cabinets. Capturing an organization's past, although a beneficial starting point for most initiatives, is not necessarily the best way to spend limited resources. A system flooded with useless information will discourage potential participants.

A key step is to conduct a content audit during the planning and design phase, which is strongly correlated with every category of improved performance in process improvement, service levels, cost savings, quality of content, and customer satisfaction. The next step is to select the appropriate approach to capturing and transferring that critical knowledge. This chapter details how to identify critical knowledge through mapping as well as common approaches for sharing it.

IDENTIFYING CRITICAL KNOWLEDGE

Several tasks can enable an organization to identify what knowledge is critical. In best-practice organizations, senior management often determines what knowledge is critical enough to capture. Interviews with employees or with subject matter experts, demographic data, participant surveys, employee turnover and tenure data, and communities of practice are also popular sources. Exit interviews may not be ideal sources, however; it may be too late to capture knowledge at the time of an employee's departure.

To identify who possesses critical knowledge, interviews with employees in changing roles and senior management discussions are again effective. Another approach for identifying who has the critical knowledge is to track the areas of critical knowledge loss by tracking attrition rates. Of course, not all knowledge is lost because of employee attrition; much is lost because employees' responsibilities shift and because projects lack a process to capture lessons learned.

The primary areas of employee loss, and hence knowledge loss, are operations and line units, information technology, research and development, and executive officers. (*Figures 3 and 4* shows results from best-practice organizations benchmarked by APQC.) APQC has also found that the knowledge management staff, as well as marketing and sales staff, are potential sources of knowledge loss for an organization.

Which Functions are Predicted to Have Potential Knowledge Loss?

Function	Percentage
Operations/Line units	77%
Information technology	77%
Research and development	55%
Marketing and sales	55%
Executive officer/team	55%
Dedicated KM staff/unit	44%
Human resources	44%
Other senior management	33%
Other	11%

Best-practice organizations (n=9)

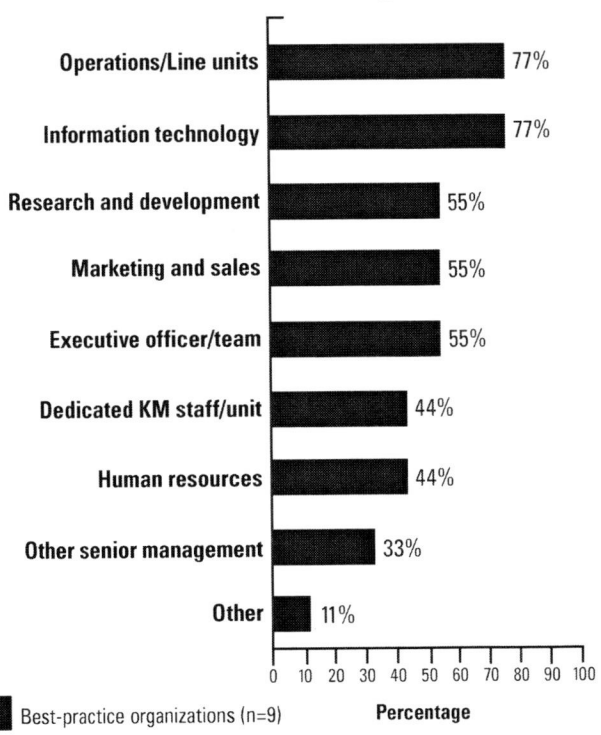

Figure 3

Specific Criteria Used to Determine What Knowledge Needs to Be Retained

Criterion	Percentage
Relevance of knowledge to business strategy	100%
Risk if knowledge is lost	89%
Timelessness of knowledge to be retained	78%
Difficulty of replacement	67%
Shelf life of knowledge to be retained	67%

Best-practice organizations (n=9)

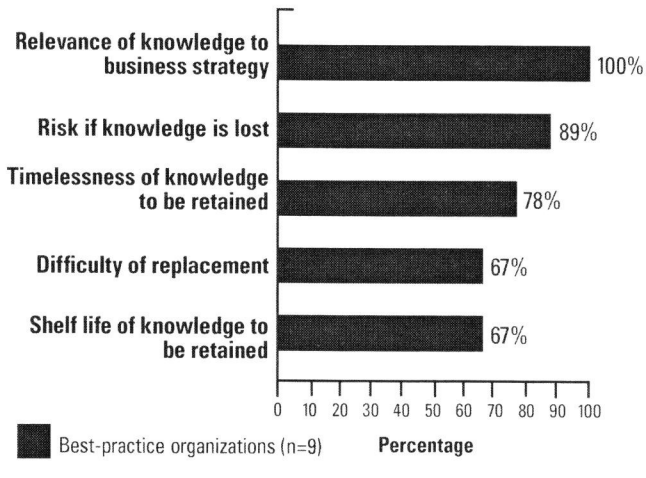

Figure 4

Once an organization has identified what knowledge needs to be retained and who has it, the next step is to determine specific criteria to assess the value of the knowledge. The relevance of the knowledge to the business strategy is usually the most important criteria. Other criteria include the uniqueness of knowledge, knowledge concerning processes, usefulness of information to customer-facing staff, and standard operating procedures.

Knowledge Maps

The following imperatives provide a step-by-step guide to identifying critical knowledge in an organization:
1. Identify the primary knowledge domains.
2. Identify the knowledge owners and/or subject matter experts.
3. Identify the knowledge bases.
4. Identify the knowledge gaps and bottlenecks.
5. Prepare information for the knowledge map.
6. Develop high-level classifications.
7. Review processes, and identify information used, generated, and needed.

8. Map the classification system, and identify knowledge used, generated, and needed.
9. Complete the inventory.

> Mapping the flow of knowledge reveals who creates the knowledge, what knowledge these creators have, and who needs it.

To retrieve critical knowledge, an organization must understand how information flows internally. Knowledge maps are pictorial depictions of an expert locator system and repositories. They also outline the relationships between the knowledge providers and the rest of the organization. Mapping the flow of knowledge reveals who creates the knowledge, what knowledge these creators have, and who needs it.

Maps capture the shared context of knowledge. Shared context is always changing, so knowledge maps are dynamic. Instead of mapping an entire domain, it is advisable to simply generate a map for a key work flow area. After selecting a process or focus area, the next step is to map the processes by determining routine and non-routine tasks, identifying key decision points and hand-offs, and locating owners and stakeholders in high-value processes. Interviews can help determine the knowledge pathways through the organization. Knowledge map creators will then make an inventory of the types of knowledge used and identify gaps, lack of connectivity, and information overload.

From these maps, an organization can determine what knowledge its employees need, where and whom they get it from, and how they use it. Also, it becomes apparent what enhances or impedes the flow and sharing of knowledge.

APPROACHES TO CAPTURE AND TRANSFER KNOWLEDGE

No single approach provides a comprehensive solution to knowledge capture and transfer. The approaches best suited for capturing and/or transferring knowledge entirely depend upon the type of knowledge an organization wants to capture and share and, more importantly, on the culture of the organization. Organizations can benefit from developing a toolkit of approaches, some of which already may be used somewhere in the organization.

SECI Model

Although some approaches to capture and share knowledge are categorically appropriate for tacit or explicit knowledge, most approaches fall somewhere on a continuum, because knowledge is dynamic. Rather than being solely tacit or explicit, it continually evolves from one state to the other. This theory is articulated in Ikujiro Nonaka's Socialization-Externalization-Combination-Internalization (SECI) model[1].

According to the SECI model, tacit and explicit knowledge interact and go through a "knowledge conversion." During this conversion, both tacit and explicit knowledge expand in quality and quantity. Knowledge conversion goes through four modes:
1. **socialization**—from tacit knowledge to tacit knowledge,
2. **externalization**—from tacit knowledge to explicit knowledge,
3. **combination**—from explicit knowledge to explicit knowledge, and
4. **internalization**—from explicit knowledge to tacit knowledge.

In *Figure 5*, page 24, APQC has placed example approaches in the four modes, based on the type of knowledge that the particular approach is most likely to capture. Although most of the approaches do not exclusively fall into any one category, they do have certain strengths in a particular category.

Communities of practice create an atmosphere for socialization where knowledge is created and shared. However, communities also fall in the combination and internalization categories because members create new explicit knowledge and enable other members to internalize knowledge, use it in their work, and then share it again with others, thus returning the cycle to socialization.

[1] Nonaka, Ikujiro, Ryoko Toyama, and Noboru Konno. *SECI, Ba and Leadership: A Unified Model of Dynamic Knowledge Creation.* Long Range Planning, vol. 33, 2000.

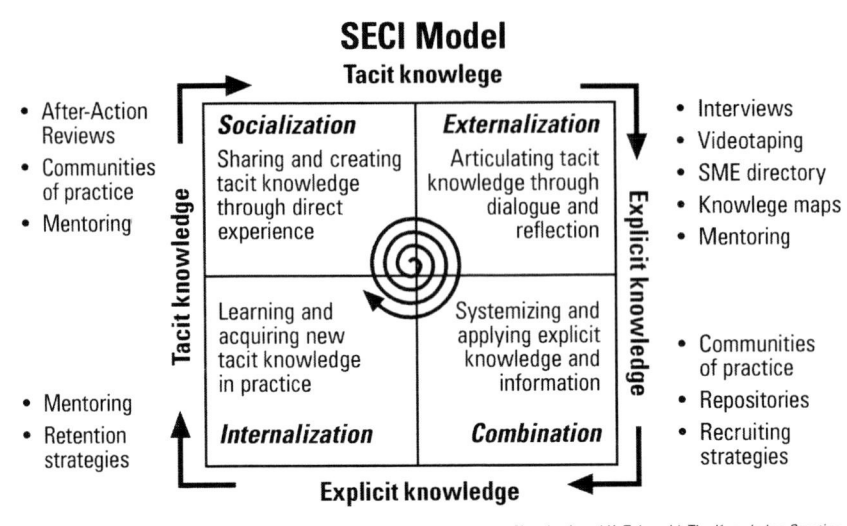

SECI Model

Tacit knowlege

- After-Action Reviews
- Communities of practice
- Mentoring

	Socialization	Externalization	
	Sharing and creating tacit knowledge through direct experience	Articulating tacit knowledge through dialogue and reflection	
	Learning and acquiring new tacit knowledge in practice	Systemizing and applying explicit knowledge and information	
	Internalization	*Combination*	

Tacit knowledge → Explicit knowledge

- Interviews
- Videotaping
- SME directory
- Knowlege maps
- Mentoring

- Communities of practice
- Repositories
- Recruiting strategies

- Mentoring
- Retention strategies

Explicit knowledge

Nonaka, I. and H. Takeuchi. *The Knowledge-Creating Company*, 1995. N.Y. Oxford Unversity Press. Adapted by APQC.

Figure 5

Interviews, knowledge maps, videotaping, After-Action Reviews, and mentoring allow individuals to convert their tacit knowledge into explicit knowledge. Therefore, these tools fall in the categories of externalization and socialization.

Repositories, expert-based systems, recruiting strategies and case-based reasoning systems fall in the combination category because they enable an organization to capture explicit knowledge and then create new knowledge based on what has already been captured. For example, a case-based reasoning system is often used by service department or call center employees. When a customer service representative receives a call, he/she researches other instances of the caller's problem or problems similar to it. The information might be an exact solution, but it is most likely that the representative and customer, through trial and error, will find another solution by manipulating the system's data. Thus, new knowledge is created by applying existing knowledge to a new experience.

Internalization refers to the actual transfer of knowledge from one person to another. Mentoring, training, and apprenticeships are all one-on-one relationships that foster the transfer of knowledge from one individual to another. The recipient of the knowledge can internalize the lessons because his/her mentor is available for guidance. In contrast, databases enable the capture of knowledge and are the means by which others in the organization get access to it. However, databases alone do not provide the atmosphere for internalizing the knowledge stored in it.

The remainder of this chapter will provide some guidance on the above-mentioned approaches for capturing, maintaining, and sharing both tacit and explicit knowledge.

Retention Strategies

Retaining employees means retaining knowledge. Although organizations rarely track attrition rates by knowledge areas, retaining employees is a fundamental solution to knowledge loss. Not all knowledge is lost when an employee leaves, but turnover does increase knowledge attrition and therefore must be addressed by both HR and the business units.

Turnover and retention rates reflect several aspects of an organization's operations. Some of the most effective organizational opportunities for retaining employees are professional development, challenging projects, and skill certification. From these opportunities, employees can continuously learn and gain new skills. It becomes a circular process: learning increases retention rates, and higher retention rates increase the knowledge of the organization.

> Retaining employees is a fundamental solution to knowledge loss.

It is also strategically advantageous to keep retirees on call or contract as consultants, mentors, and/or advisers. This extended retention strategy is targeted at functional areas of industrial trades, engineering, executive level, and technical experts. In most cases, no financial compensation is involved.

It is important to note that attrition is not always bad. New employees bring new ideas and new perspectives to an organization.

After-Action Reviews

The After-Action Review, a technique created by the U.S. Army, provides teams with feedback by reflecting on their activities, with a focus on performance standards *(Figure 6)*. Consequently, the organization gains explicit lessons learned, and the team learns its strengths and weaknesses in performance.

After-Action Reviews and the Project Planning Process

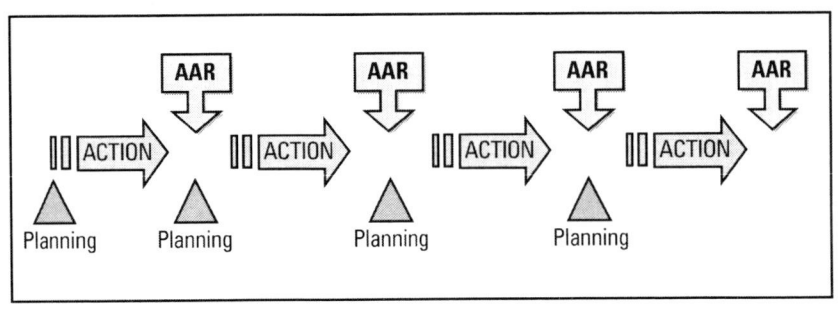

Signet Consulting Group, 2000

Figure 6

Although After-Action Reviews cultivate and categorize explicit knowledge, the greatest value from an After-Action Review comes from the tacit transfer of knowledge during the post-activity review. Participants determine what was supposed to happen, what actually happened, and what they learned. A review to share insights and discuss how goals were met need not only be held at the end of a large and/or formal project; an After-Action Review can be held after any identifiable event within a project's time frame. At that time, memory is fresh and unvarnished, and the participants are usually still available. Lessons can be applied immediately.

To conduct an After-Action Review, the Army typically:
- reviews first what the unit or team intended to accomplish (the overall mission or objective);

- establishes the "ground truth" of what actually took place through a moment-by-moment replay of critical events;
- explores potential causes of actual results by focusing on one or more key issues;
- allows unit or team members to articulate what they should learn from the review, including what they did well and what needs improvement; and
- concludes with a preview of the next project and issues that might arise.

All activity participants should be involved to gain multiple viewpoints; a singular point of view is more like a critique. The role of the After-Action Review supervisor is to focus on trends, not individuals.

> The role of the After-Action Review supervisor is to focus on trends, not individuals.

Mentoring

The mentor/protégé relationship facilitates the transfer of knowledge from experienced employees, such as subject matter experts, to employees new to the organization or a department. Such programs focus on leadership, behavior, and skill development, especially for high-potential employees. Tacit knowledge transferred might include orientation to the organization's culture. Explicit knowledge could include specific job tools and processes.

A successful mentoring relationship provides benefits to both parties by expanding their knowledge, skills, energy, and creativity. For the purposes of knowledge retention, mentoring programs effectively transfer knowledge from a leaving employee to a successor.

The first step is to identify the areas within the organization that may benefit from mentoring. HR can help to identify individuals (traditionally junior employees) open to feedback and coaching. Mentors should be assigned to protégés, because protégés allowed to choose their own mentor would likely pick someone like themselves. This would not foster diversity and differences in ideas and opinions.

> Find concentrated pockets of potentially
> retiring employees for immediate attention.

Organizations that use internal mentors typically look to their high-middle to top-level managers. External mentors tend to be identified as successful in their profession. They may be recruited through a professional association. Internal mentors should be selected from outside the employee's immediate work area.

Participants should receive approval from their supervisors because the mentor/protégé relationship requires a time commitment. Mentors and protégés must be given ample opportunities to meet and share information, both in a formal work setting, as well as in an informal environment.

It is possible that the mentor/protégé relationship will not prove enjoyable or beneficial. Therefore, it may need to be re-evaluated after a set time span. It is critical for the relationship to be monitored, typically by an HR representative. Success is more likely if the mentor understands the objectives of the program so he/she can guide the protégé accordingly. The mentor should understand that the role will involve:
- familiarizing the protégé with the work environment,
- fostering creative thinking,
- guiding the protégé through difficult situations,
- building the self-confidence of the protégé,
- acting as a source of information and encouragement, and
- providing career guidance.

For this involvement, mentors should receive recognition. Although mentors receive intrinsic rewards by nurturing another employee and helping him/her grow professionally, tangible rewards such as extended vacation time or extra pay shows a commitment of support on the part of the organization. A sure sign of a mentor's success is when a protégé volunteers to become a mentor for someone else.

The success of a mentoring program is difficult to measure in resolute terms. The transfer of tacit knowledge is impossible to codify in its entirety, and the only means of measuring the effectiveness of a mentoring relationship is either by attributing increased retention rates of employees or by monitoring the success of the protégé. This typically requires a strong relationship between business units and HR departments so that these changes can be monitored and attributed at least in part to the mentoring program.

Interviews

Interviews to capture knowledge are typically conducted during a project review or prior to the departure of an employee from the company or from his/her current position. Few organizations use this approach. However, it can be a very effective means to capture tacit knowledge. Although information in an interview is shared verbally, it can be made explicit and stored in a repository for future use.

In addition to the types of interviews cited in **Figure 7** by APQC study participants, organizations may benefit from oral history interviews, strategic competence management interviews, and subject matter expert interviews. Interviews also can be conducted

What Types of Interviews Do You Conduct?

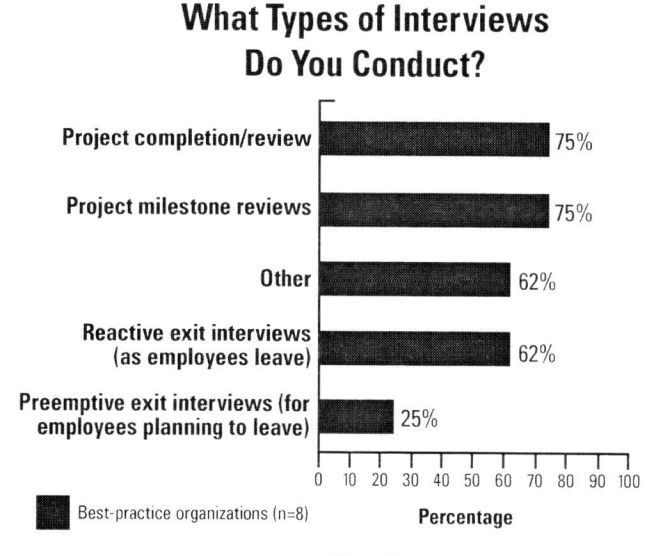

Interview Type	Percentage
Project completion/review	75%
Project milestone reviews	75%
Other	62%
Reactive exit interviews (as employees leave)	62%
Preemptive exit interviews (for employees planning to leave)	25%

Best-practice organizations (n=8)

Figure 7

after a tour of duty in a country office, after mission-critical or innovative work, and after special projects or pilot projects.

The first step is to find concentrated pockets of potentially retiring employees for immediate attention. Subject matter experts, as well as key players in special projects and senior employees, are also ideal candidates. An invitation should be extended only after the employee's supervisor has approved the projected time commitment.

If the employee is willing to participate, an interview should be organized for an informal setting, with a subject matter expert. In the case of a departing employee, the interviewer could be his/her successor. A departing employee, especially one making a quick exit, may not want to collaborate with a supervisor but may be open to sharing knowledge with colleagues and/or peers. A best-case scenario is to have the recipient of the information be the one to conduct the interview. This is because in an interview, tacit knowledge is transferred directly to the interviewer. This knowledge may be lost if the interviewer then has to transfer it to the recipient.

Videotaping may be an option; it allows for a richer capture of the knowledge. It allows the interviewer to capture more of the context, as well as tone and body language (unless the interviewee is nervous in front of the camera). On the other hand, videotaped interviews can be cumbersome for recipients if they are long and cannot be searched by content. Videotapes can be indexed and delivered online, but bandwidth and post-production costs can be a prohibiting factor.

The number of interviews conducted can be used as a measure of activity concerning the quantity of knowledge captured.

Communities of Practice

Communities are an effective approach to capturing and sharing tacit knowledge. APQC has seen the concept of communities evolve from informal groups that network together to formal groups with goals and accountability. APQC defines communities of practice as groups of people who share and learn from one another face-to-face and virtually. They are held together by a common interest in a body of knowledge and are driven by a desire and need to share problems, experiences, insights, templates, tools, and best practices.

> APQC has seen the concept of communities
> evolve from informal groups that network together
> to formal groups with goals and accountability.

The first step to create a formal CoP is to search for existing, informal communities in the organization. If the focus of the community is related to a key business goal and an executive would be willing to sponsor the community, approach a community member and introduce the idea of formalizing the community and some of its activities. Select a member who appears to be a knowledge sharer; an individual with a passion for the topic is often willing to invest time and effort to see a community gain organizational influence.

If there is no natural core group leading the community, create a design team to determine the best means of communication, how often the community meets, whether it is face-to-face or virtual, and the topic or theme of the meeting. The design team lays the ground rules and even some measures to determine whether or not the community will be successful. In some organizations, design teams are overseen by either steering committees or advisory boards that provide the community with senior leadership support and visibility in the organization.

The next step is to organize a face-to-face meeting with community members. Many people mistakenly believe that electronic or online interaction is enough to form relationships among employees. A best-case scenario for a community is to have at least one face-to-face meeting so that members can meet. If possible, aim to have the community meet face-to-face at least once or twice a year, if not more regularly.

The community is now prepared to facilitate knowledge retention. As the community captures knowledge, a repository should be designed to store the community's explicit knowledge so it can be disseminated across the organization, if applicable.

Throughout the process, communities need to be flexible in order to evolve easily. Too much attention is just as hazardous as too little attention, because communities that feel too much pressure to

> Too much attention is just as hazardous as too little attention, because communities that feel too much pressure to perform quickly dissipate.

perform quickly dissipate. Cross-functional support—such as IT, change management, and HR—is necessary to sustain productivity. Successful communities have time to grow before trying to measure their own effectiveness.

As communities become a more integral part of the organization, they begin to reshape the organization by changing the culture to one of greater knowledge sharing. Not only does this approach capture and transfer existing critical knowledge, but it also becomes a significant resource for realizing new competitive advantages.

Subject Matter Experts Directories

A directory can be as simple as an organization's phone list. With the advent of HR systems that track employee information, yellow pages or directories can locate experts, both inside and outside the organization. The yellow pages, directories, or expert locator systems are primarily used for the exchange of tacit knowledge. The only explicit part of the data capture is attaining information about the expert. These tools allow access to humans, rather than to information, to enable an actual conversation or e-mail exchange that provides the context for information.

Information for the directory is fed by or built on the existing corporate HR system. If this system is in a word processing document or spreadsheet, then it will need to be converted into a relational database so that information can be sorted and individuals can be linked to their topic of expertise. If the directory exists in an HR software system, often called an expert locator system, the system's capabilities should be extended to include areas of expertise. The challenge is to build a hierarchy of skills and competencies, while respecting the original security limitation of the information.

An organization that creates an SME directory from scratch can more easily structure the directory to their specification but should expect a lengthier time commitment to understand user requirements, map requirements to the software's functionality, motivate experts to supply their profiles, and conduct milestone reviews. In this approach, it is best to start small but leave options open for expansion. Because most expert directories are self-policed, best-practice organizations typically do not spend a lot of time designing expert verification processes.

Repositories

Document repositories are structured content, such as alphanumeric data. Whereas databases hold information, repositories include a portal that structures and categorizes knowledge. Without a repository, the proliferation of isolated databases within an organization makes it difficult for employees to fuse knowledge.

Repositories are used primarily to capture explicit information. Many repositories contain databases that focus on customer information, such as inquiries, needs and interactions, and databases that contain competitor intelligence. These databases typically include sales presentations, reports, customer engagement information, competitor analysis, and external feeds.

One of the challenges is integrating different portals and databases that contain particular types of information. The best repository systems automatically capture content, rather than require users to re-enter it. Users are then drawn to this reference tool by its magnet content, such as information on sales and solution support or external resources for information related to the employee's business area or area of expertise.

Every system needs a disciplined process for creation, evaluation, categorization, maintenance, and renewal of information to maintain user levels. To ensure a proper structure and avoid inaccuracy, poor subject matter knowledge, and inaccurate categorizations, organizations should employ library scientists who understand the technology and technologists who understand library science. Editorial and publishing support increases the accuracy of information stored in the repository. Automatic systems keep the repository clean and current. Submitting the data is the easy part. Retrieving the data is typically based on how a user thinks the data is classified—that is the hard part.

The number of repositories in an organization can be mind boggling, because every function, project, product, or person seems to require its own repository. Introducing a knowledge management repository adds one more to the pool. Therefore, it is beneficial to leverage the use of existing information before creating new information. A knowledge repository should link to other repositories in the organization so that employees can access many knowledge pools from one spot. If the information is not structured and classified well, individuals will not be able to locate it, and the repository will lose credibility.

> It is beneficial to leverage the use of existing information before creating new information.

E-mail

Although its ability to capture knowledge is limited by privacy procedures, e-mail is the most frequently used approach for knowledge transfer. For knowledge sharing, it is widely considered only moderately effective, in part because it acts as a tacit knowledge transfer tool. Information may be written down, but it is not categorized or stored in a common repository and is usually an informal expression of a person's thoughts and ideas about a subject.

Previously mentioned transfer tools—such as communities of practice, face-to-face meetings, and dedicated knowledge management repositories—are considered more effective.

However, e-mails are effective knowledge-sharing tools in that, unlike other approaches, they are used daily and are often primarily event-driven. Databases, on the other hand, are difficult to build into an employee's work flow unless the system is designed exactly around an employee's work processes.

CONCLUSION

Internal networks, the documentation of the work flow/process (i.e., repositories), and project milestone reviews are the most frequently used approaches for capturing tacit knowledge. APQC has found that the most effective approaches at best-practice organizations are project milestone reviews, communities of practice and internal networks, After-Action Reviews, conferences for knowledge sharing, and interviews.

For explicit knowledge, best-practice organizations rely heavily on collaboration tools for capturing explicit knowledge; use of these tools is part of employees' work flow or daily activities. Other tools used to capture explicit knowledge include content management systems, document management systems, and shared folders or drives. The most effective approaches to capture explicit data are communities of practice workspaces, engagement team databases, decision support systems, and collaboration tools.

For knowledge transfer, the most effective approaches are communities of practice, face-to-face team or department meetings, e-mail, one-on-one consultation with an expert, and apprenticeship programs. With the exception of e-mail, all of these approaches involve a face-to-face component.

Figure 8, page 36, groups the aforementioned approaches into four categories: embedded in existing work processes, project related, ongoing group discussions, and one on one. The second column shows the primary frequency of use for each approach at surveyed best-practice organizations. The third column shows the average percentage of best-practice organization questionnaire respondents that use each approach.

The challenge in identifying, capturing, and transferring critical knowledge is to scale the approach to the desired quality of personal interaction. This will involve answering the following questions: What is the problem? What groups will benefit most (and consequently receive the information first)? What approaches will best suit the way people work in the organization? Will people respond better to an approach that is personal rather than technical? Are the employees technologically savvy? Are the resources to implement new technology available? Can existing technology be leveraged? And is a support structure in place for the knowledge retention efforts?

Approaches to capture and transfer knowledge are only one piece of the puzzle. They have to be supported by senior management and employees in order to succeed.

Approaches

	Daily, Weekly, Monthly Quarterly, Annually, Event Driven, NA/Not Used	Percentage Used
Embedded in existing work processes		
E-mail	Daily	88%
	NA/Not used	8%
Face-to-face department or team meetings	Weekly	40%
Teleconferences	Event-driven	48%
Videoconferences	Event-driven	60%
Training	Weekly	16%
	Annually	16%
	Event-driven	44%
Project related		
After-Action Reviews	Event-driven	60%
	NA/Not used	36%
Written reports/ Project summaries	Event-driven	64%
	NA/Not used	12%
Ongoing group discussions		
Communities of practice	Event-driven	24%
	NA/Not used	24%
Threaded discussion forums	NA/Not used	52%
Special activities	Event-driven	36%
Internal benchmarking exercises	NA/Not used	44%
Dedicated KM repository for best practices	Daily	24%
	NA/Not used	48%
One on one		
One-on-one consultation (with an expert)	Event-driven	64%
	NA/Not used	12%
One-on-one consultation (through a help desk function)	Event-driven	40%
	NA/Not used	28%
Mentoring programs	Event-driven	32%
	NA/Not used	44%
Apprenticeship programs	Event-driven	24%
	NA/Not used	56%

Figure 8

— Chapter 4 —

Support Structures and Funding

Knowledge retention, like knowledge management, does not occur in a vacuum. It needs a support framework to define, direct, and maintain it. Many organizations are addressing this need by leveraging existing knowledge management structures, relationships, skills, and tools to develop their knowledge retention initiatives. This chapter provides an overview of the key elements of a generic support model for knowledge retention, what roles or functions the initiative requires to keep it thriving and energized, and the levels of funding needed for its maintenance and ongoing development.

SUPPORT STRUCTURES

APQC defines knowledge management support structures as the organizational groups or networks created at a corporate and/or a functional level that link to an organization's formal structure and provide the direction, processes, and resources an initiative needs to grow and sustain itself over time.

Although the support structures vary from organization to organization, three critical elements are present in successful knowledge retention initiatives:
1. senior management support (an advisory board or steering committee),
2. a central knowledge management support group, and
3. the involvement of various business units or functions.

Members of one group might also participate in another group (e.g., an executive may serve on both the advisory board and the steering committee). Not every organization has both an executive steering committee and an advisory board; however, both are described here in order to provide a better understanding of the options available. The key difference between this and other knowledge management models is the presence of the business units or functions.

Executive Steering Committee

Senior management support continues to be a significant factor in knowledge retention initiatives. Usually a cross-functional team made up of members of senior management, the steering committee validates knowledge management and retention activities and sets the direction. Steering committees fund projects, as well as minimize barriers and promote knowledge sharing throughout the enterprise. The steering committee ensures that the business units, corporate, and IT are working in the same direction with the same scope.

Advisory Board

Like a steering committee, the advisory board is a cross-functional team with senior-level executives and advisers. The advisory board directs the strategic alignment, prioritizes projects, resolves KM issues and needs, communicates KM messages and successes, and supports communities of practice and collaboration methods for transfer of high-value tacit knowledge. Embedded within theses highly visible responsibilities are the tasks to create, capture, and leverage knowledge management best practices and approaches and advocate and support common processes for knowledge access, management, and use.

Central Knowledge Management Group

Because knowledge retention is typically part of an overall knowledge management strategy, organizations rarely have a separate knowledge retention implementation team. Knowledge management practitioners—including the core KM team, HR and training personnel, IT personnel, and business owners—manage the actual design, development, and deployment of knowledge retention initiatives. This group must also cultivate the knowledge management strategy and infrastructure to support knowledge sharing.

It is important to note the presence of IT and HR or training personnel. After its initial contribution during the development of the initiative, IT's continued involvement enables the KM group

> Organizations rarely have a separate knowledge retention implementation team.

to take advantage of technologies already available within the organization and to gain immediate feedback on technology-related decisions. HR's involvement strengthens the organization's recruiting, training, and retention efforts by retaining critical business knowledge.

Business owners are frequently involved in the KM group because they see firsthand the need to prevent the loss of critical-to-business knowledge. In many cases in large organizations, representatives from this group do not volunteer to join the knowledge management group, so the team has to seek them out. However, once they realize the value of the knowledge retention approaches, they usually begin to approach the KM group on their own.

The amount of time dedicated to knowledge retention initiatives varies by role, function, and organization. In most cases, employees focus on knowledge retention initiatives in addition to their regular responsibilities. The number of full-time employees for each role or function also varies. Experienced KM practitioners use existing skills and tools, along with previous lessons learned, to develop their knowledge retention initiatives, therefore requiring time for the role.

KNOWLEDGE RETENTION ROLES

Knowledge retention roles fall into two categories: core roles and approach-specific roles.

Core roles tie back directly to the central knowledge management group. Although the team make-up varies among organizations, the following core roles are pervasive in best-practice initiatives:

- **leader**—responsible for the strategic direction of and investments for the knowledge management team;
- **knowledge management team members**—support various business owners or product groups in their knowledge retention efforts through advice, funding, meeting facilitation, and technology and personnel support;

- **HR/training personnel**—may contribute information, align strategies, and provide training;
- **IT personnel**—enable immediate feedback on potential IT approaches and can handle related requests from knowledge users;
- **business owner or product group representatives**—can familiarize the knowledge management team with the experiences of outward-facing groups and generate buy-in and visibility for the various knowledge retention approaches on the front lines; and
- **content managers**—support and maintain repositories and content management systems, as well as adhere to the organization's security classification and records management procedures.

Approach-specific roles are not needed on a daily basis. These roles or functions may have been developed specifically for a particular approach. For example, a videographer will be needed only for interviews. The following positions and roles may support the central knowledge management group as needed:

- subject matter expert,
- business owner,
- tactical HR representative,
- administrative support,
- videographer,
- interviewer,
- gatekeeper,
- CoP leader,
- CoP administrator,
- database administrator,
- project manager, and
- taxonomy specialist.

Again, the amount of time dedicated to a knowledge retention initiative varies by role and organization. Depending on the approaches used to capture and transfer knowledge, new roles or functions may be needed to support the knowledge retention initiatives.

FUNDING

Knowledge retention initiatives need sufficient resources to fulfill their purpose. Resources include start-up costs, training, facilitation, and leader and member time. In many cases, organizations are able to build on the knowledge management tools and skills already in place. Therefore, some funding comes from budgets or allocations already

> In many cases, organizations are able to build on the knowledge management tools and skills already in place. Therefore, some funding comes from budgets or allocations already in existence.

in existence. Some knowledge retention activities focus more on HR and business units or functions, so these entities provide more funding for knowledge retention activities than previously seen. (*Figure 9*, page 42, shows results from a recent APQC benchmarking study.) Because knowledge loss reaches into all levels of the organization, funding for these initiatives is coming from new sources (i.e., HR, research and development, and operation or line units), which allows the knowledge management team to share the burden of supporting these knowledge retention initiatives.

The cost of a knowledge retention initiative typically ranges from $100,000 to $249,000. The average range spent by leading organizations for the maintenance and ongoing development of their knowledge retention initiatives is considerably lower where a KM initiative is already established.

Strategies, approaches and tools, support structures, and funding are critical for a successful knowledge retention initiative. However, like any strategic initiative, knowledge retention will not work if employees are not committed to its success.

Functions Providing Funding for Knowledge Retention Initiative in Organization

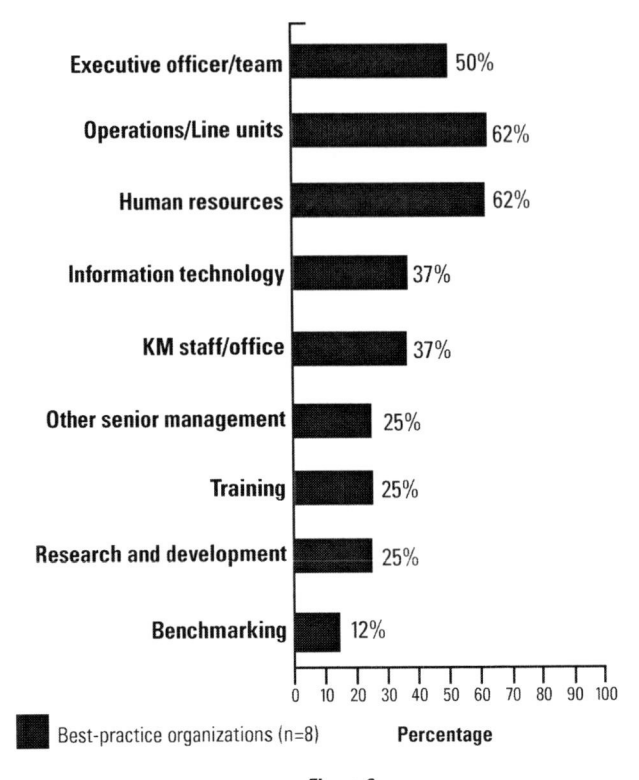

Function	Percentage
Executive officer/team	50%
Operations/Line units	62%
Human resources	62%
Information technology	37%
KM staff/office	37%
Other senior management	25%
Training	25%
Research and development	25%
Benchmarking	12%

■ Best-practice organizations (n=8)   Percentage

Figure 9

— Chapter 5 —

Critical Success Factors

Effective knowledge retention is based on an organization's willingness and ability to share knowledge. Employees justifiably need a reason to change the way they work, and awareness and tools are necessary to successfully retain knowledge through improved work processes.

The key enablers to facilitating organizational knowledge sharing and retention are: awareness and communication, formal endorsement by senior management, involvement in communities of practice, and the use of the training function. Communication and awareness strategies are employed more widely than senior management directives, which attests to the importance of word-of-mouth communications and the benefits of seeing others participate. Communities of practice provide a forum and medium for knowledge capture and transfer, and training activities build knowledge sharing into employees' skill sets and daily work flow.

A number of critical success factors come into play during the implementation of a knowledge retention initiative.

- **Communication**—A critical enabler of effective implementation is clear communication, especially from the executive level. A declaration of strong management support provides an incentive for people to collaborate and share. It is important to identify stakeholders that must receive communication and to include daily, weekly, and monthly communication ideas, as well as key leadership messages. (These messages must be adapted to the audience.) Best-practice organizations use all company media to disseminate the message and cascade the communication plans throughout the organization.

- **Executive support**—An organization with executive support can implement an effective knowledge retention initiative much more quickly. In fact, grassroots initiatives take at least two more years to develop, with time needed to build the business case, develop champions, and secure resources. Not surprisingly, those organizations with initiatives beginning as an enterprise directive had the resources, buy-in, and burning issue (sense of urgency) needed to start development immediately.

- **Involvement of human resources**—Best-practice organizations exhibit strategic partnerships between the human resources function and core business strategies. If retaining and sharing knowledge is a key feature of the human resources system, knowledge management activities will demonstrate ties to: organizational learning, recruiting and retention, training activities, rewards and recognition, and mentoring programs.

- **Rewards and recognition**—Individuals who share and retain knowledge can better perform their jobs and consequently receive recognition as key contributors and experts. Often, organizations need to create more structured reward and recognition systems to encourage employees to change their behavior. A standardized reward system may help institutionalize the practice into the common culture. Behavior that is rewarded is repeated.

  People desire status and want to be valued for what they know. Recognition lies in being perceived as an expert by employees and management. This may involve attaching an author's name to documents, guidelines, and presentations or celebrating best practices success stories. If those who share and receive knowledge do not feel rewarded, they likely won't provide the desired results.

  Using the knowledge system has to be self-rewarding to the consumer as well; users have to get something out of it, be it knowledge they need or a sense of status and recognition. Formal rewards are never as frequent, and rarely as valuable, as the rewards embedded in the activity itself.

> Often, organizations need to create more structured reward and recognition systems to encourage employees to change their behavior.

- **Measurement**—Measures can assess an organization's knowledge retention progress and provide vital information about strategies for achieving its goals. At every stage, measurement can focus attention on desired behaviors and results. Responsibility for the measurement process lies primarily within the knowledge management team.

  The most effective method to measure the success of knowledge retention is to track activities in which knowledge is captured. Taking user surveys and tracking the number of interviews are also effective methods. It is much more difficult to calculate the value of retained knowledge. The most effective methods to measure the success of knowledge transfer are conducting user surveys, tracking the number of knowledge objects accessed and used, and tracking knowledge transfer activities. Tracking requests for information and hits on knowledge-sharing Web pages, assessing anecdotal evidence, and conducting surveys also help to assess the effectiveness of knowledge retention initiatives.

- **Collaborative working environments**—Modifying the physical office setting can beneficially alter the structure of work groups. Easier access to information and expertise facilitates the exchange and flow of knowledge. Changing the physical office environment can improve knowledge sharing, social networks and trust, team productivity, collaboration and communication, space utilization, and employee satisfaction.

Effecting change in an organization is not easy. Yet, employees who understand the need for and value of change are more willing to try a new process. Stress that new processes related to knowledge retention can improve the daily work flow for employees and make their jobs easier. Measurement processes, HR involvement, communication and executive support strategies, and reward and recognition programs can smooth the path of resistance to change on the knowledge management journey.

— Chapter 6 —

Conclusion

This book addresses the need to identify and capture valuable knowledge before it is lost. Knowledge retention activities have a unique challenge within the knowledge management arena. Encouraging contribution is a challenge for any knowledge management initiative, but it has a slightly different twist in a retention context: the individuals who need to contribute may be leaving the organization or the project. The appropriate time to initiate a knowledge retention initiative is before massive loss or turnover is imminent; however, if the loss isn't looming, it can be hard to convince management to provide resources. Therefore, organizations must build a comprehensive knowledge retention system to capture knowledge, even in unpredicted scenarios. This system involves:

- building a knowledge-sharing culture in the organization,
- preparing new hires quickly,
- capturing valuable knowledge as employees leave the organization,
- organizing project reviews,
- preventing the loss of technical knowledge, and
- providing newer/less experienced employees access to more experienced/knowledgeable employees.

Organizations leading the path in knowledge retention have provided APQC with some prevalent lessons learned.

- The best way to retain valuable knowledge in the face of attrition or downsizing is to build and sustain systemic knowledge management approaches.
- To identify what knowledge is critical to capture, discussions with senior management, communities of practice, and interviews with employees or subject matter experts are effective approaches. Interviewing departing employees may be too late to capture knowledge.
- Determine what knowledge is critical by assessing its relevance to the business strategy.

- The most effective way to capture, retain, and transfer valuable knowledge is to embed that process into the work flow in a conscious and disciplined approach. This not only retains the context, but also links the sources and co-creators of knowledge while they are still present to learn from one another. Examples include project/milestone reviews, After-Action Reviews, team meetings, and communities of practice. After-the-fact tacit knowledge codification is better than nothing, but it loses the richness of context and dialogue; it is critical to facilitate people-to-people learning or tacit knowledge transfer during the process itself.
- The "capture" of tacit knowledge—the most valuable and difficult knowledge to distil in any organization—is best retained through communities of practice and networks.

> The most effective way to capture, retain, and transfer valuable knowledge is to embed that process into the work flow in a conscious and disciplined approach.

- There is no unquestionably superior application or technology for knowledge retention. Most organizations use basic tools, such as collaborative applications, data repositories, e-mail, and videoconferencing.
- Best-practice organizations typically have three critical elements in their knowledge management and retention support structures: senior management support, a central knowledge management support group, and the involvement of different business units/functions in the initiative. Strong, active support from senior-level executives and an ongoing knowledge management group are essential.
- The reported costs for knowledge retention initiatives are less than previously seen for knowledge management initiatives in APQC's experience, apparently because best-practice organizations build on existing tools and skills and often build retention activities into the existing work flow.

- The knowledge management team should work closely with the human resources team to design and implement knowledge retention strategies, including hiring employees who will work effectively in a knowledge-sharing environment.
- Best-practice organizations measure the effectiveness of knowledge retention initiatives through a variety of methods. The most effective methods to measure the success of knowledge transfer are conducting user surveys, tracking the number of knowledge objects accessed and used, tracking knowledge transfer activities, and capturing meaningful stories of the power of knowledge capture and transfer.
- Best-practice organizations demonstrate a link between knowledge management and organizational learning. Take valuable knowledge captured and embed it into the learning process.
- Knowledge loss, like knowledge creation, is a continuous dynamic. Not all knowledge should be captured. Therefore, the knowledge retention initiative must be focused on critical knowledge that creates value for the organization. One way best-practice organizations ensure they target the right knowledge is to link their knowledge retention efforts to a specific domain and to use executives and subject matter experts to identify key knowledge.
- Videotaping and interviewing are both highly effective means of tacit knowledge capture. If videotaped interviews are so effective, why are they not used more? The explanation may be hidden in the cost and effort required to render lengthy interview information searchable and retrievable. It is relatively easy to videotape an interview, but it is labor-intensive to edit and catalog the video archive. Furthermore, bandwidth limitations may make access difficult or impossible. Videotaping is very effective for capturing organizational history and stories or general lessons learned about a client, but the process and technology for making videotaped interviews fully searchable remains elusive. Likewise, interview notes may capture valuable instruction and lessons learned. But unless they are searchable, it may be very difficult to effectively disseminate the results.

- After-Action Reviews have been highly touted and widely documented in business literature for several years. Virtually any organization can organize project milestone reviews to capture lessons for a knowledge retention effort.
- The most effective approaches have a personal or face-to-face element. Both communities and networks are very effective and popular approaches, which underscores that tacit knowledge is contextual and social and is more effectively captured and shared through collaborative interaction.

Systematic knowledge sharing, capture, and transfer are keys to effective knowledge retention. The most effective knowledge retention approaches are systematic, ingrained, and behavioral—not merely transactional knowledge-capture exercises. APQC believes that knowledge retention will also be the key to future innovation.

> The most effective knowledge retention approaches are systematic, ingrained, and behavioral—not merely transactional knowledge-capture exercises.

Organizational innovation usually results from the pressure to adapt and change. In the heat of battle or when facing customer demands, employees invent solutions that work. Improvisation leads to innovation. New technologies, demographics, a vision of how things might be, and a passion for new possibilities also drive innovation.

How can organizations leverage, share, and build on these drivers and become more innovative?

The best advice is to work toward creating systematic and systemic approaches that will build organizational capabilities to retain valuable knowledge in any climate. If your organization faces an imminent loss of valuable knowledge, then target the knowledge loss as an initial, high-priority, and high-payoff knowledge management project and roll the lessons learned and methodologies into future activities.

About the Authors

Alice Haytmanek

Alice Haytmanek has worked with APQC since 2000, conducting consortium benchmarking studies and providing implementation assistance to a wide variety of organizations. With a focus on K–12 education, e-learning, and leadership development, Haytmanek spearheaded the Broad Foundation Benchmarking Project.

Haytmanek's previous experience includes teaching at the middle-school level and developing and facilitating workshops as a career consultant at Georgetown University.

She holds a bachelor's degree in psychology from Bucknell University in Pennsylvania and a master's degree in education and human development from the George Washington University.

Paige Leavitt

An editor and writer, Paige Leavitt helped to produce a number of APQC publications, including Best-practice Reports and the Passport to Success series.

Before joining APQC, Leavitt edited language arts textbooks for Holt, Rinehart & Winston. Leavitt has a bachelor's degree in English from the University of Texas at Austin.

Darcy Lemons

Darcy Lemons is a project manager with APQC. She manages consortium and individual studies, collects and analyzes data, and creates benchmarking reports. Project manager for the recent Retaining Valuable Knowledge consortium benchmarking study, Lemons' other recent studies have focused on best practices in e-learning and KM innovation.

Prior to joining APQC, Lemons worked in the retail industry for several years. She last held the position of assistant manager of merchandising for Barnes & Noble Booksellers. Lemons also worked as a research assistant at Texas Tech University.

Lemons earned a bachelor's degree in psychology at Texas Tech University, graduating magna cum laude. She continued her education at Texas Tech for three more years, earning a master's degree in interdisciplinary studies (education psychology, family psychology, and psychology) and graduating with honors.

About APQC

An internationally recognized resource for process and performance improvement, the American Productivity & Quality Center (APQC) helps organizations adapt to rapidly changing environments, build new and better ways to work, and succeed in a competitive marketplace.

With a focus on benchmarking, knowledge management, metrics, performance measurement, and quality improvement initiatives, APQC works with its member organizations to identify best practices, discover effective methods of improvement, broadly disseminate findings, and connect individuals with one another and the knowledge, training, and tools they need to succeed. Founded in 1977, APQC is a member-based nonprofit serving organizations around the world in all sectors of business, education, and government.

APQC offers a variety of products and services including:
- consortium, custom, and metric benchmarking studies;
- publications, including books, Best-practice Reports, and implementation guides;
- computer-based, on-site, and custom training;
- consulting and facilitation services; and
- networking opportunities.

To find out more about APQC, call 800-776-9676 (or 713-681-4020 outside the United States) or visit www.apqc.org.